Religious Politics

by
Roberts Liardon

EMBASSY
PUBLISHING

Unless otherwise indicated, all Scripture quotations are taken from the *King James Version* of the Bible.

5th Printing
Over 72,500 in Print

Religious Politics
ISBN 1-879993-02-3

P.O. Box 30710
Laguna Hills, CA 92654

Published by Embassy Publishing
P. O. Box 3500
Laguna Hills, CA 92654

Religious Politics

Killers of Ministries

Most Christians know that there are three major killers of ministries — money, pride, and sex — and ministries have fallen victim to these "killers" throughout the centuries. Ministries that were supposed to rock the nations and make the history books were never able to rock even a local community, because they fell before they could stand.

People have heard so much teaching on the dangers of ministers falling because of money, pride, and sex that they don't listen anymore. They think they're exempt. But no one is exempt. *As long as you're living, you're not exempt!*

Of course, it is normal to want financial security, respect, and a happy marriage. But there is a right way — God's way — to achieve these goals so they won't destroy you.

Religious politics is the fourth killer of ministries. I rarely preach on it, because the first three killers destroy so many ministries. However, in this book I want to help those who are willing to take the extra precautions necessary to save their ministries from this fourth killer.

The Church is so full of religious politics today that it's not just taking place behind closed doors among the pastoral staff; it's everywhere. Religious politics is the real reason there is fighting within religious organizations and among ministers, whether they are well known or not.

The first thing to understand is that ministers will find themselves with many opportunities to participate in religious politics; especially after they achieve a certain degree of success in the natural. At this point, they may enter the door of religious politics if they don't know better, or if they are not secure enough in their relationship with God. To gain some Biblical insight into this problem, turn to First Kings 22.

> **And it came to pass...that Jehoshaphat the king of Judah came down to the king of Israel....**
>
> **And Jehoshaphat said unto the king of Israel, Inquire, I pray thee, at the word of the Lord to day.**
>
> **Then the king of Israel gathered the prophets together, about four hundred men, and said unto them, Shall I go against Ramothgilead to battle, or shall I forbear? And they said, Go up; for the Lord shall deliver it into the hand of the king.**
>
> **And Jehoshaphat said, Is there not here a prophet of the Lord besides, that we might inquire of him?**
>
> **And the king of Israel said unto Jehoshaphat, There is yet one man, Micaiah the son of Imlah, by whom we**

may inquire of the Lord: but I hate him; for he doth not prophesy good concerning me, but evil. And Jehoshaphat said, Let not the king say so.

Then the king of Israel called an officer, and said, Hasten hither Micaiah the son of Imlah.

And the king of Israel and Jehoshaphat the king of Judah sat each on his throne, having put on their robes, in a void place in the entrance of the gate of Samaria; and all the prophets prophesied before them....

And the messenger that was gone to call Micaiah spake unto him, saying, Behold now, the words of the prophets declare good unto the king with one mouth: let thy word, I pray thee, be like the word of one of them, and speak that which is good.

And Micaiah said, As the Lord liveth, what the Lord saith unto me, that will I speak.

So he came to the king. And the king [of Israel] said unto him, Micaiah, shall we go against Ramoth-gilead to battle, or shall we forbear? And he answered him, Go, and prosper: for the Lord shall deliver it into the hand of the king.

And the king said unto him, How many times shall I adjure thee that thou tell me nothing but that which is true in the name of the Lord?

And he said, I saw all Israel scattered upon the hills, as sheep that have not a shepherd: and the Lord said, These have no master. . . .

And the king of Israel said unto Jehoshaphat, Did I not tell thee that he would prophesy no good concerning me, but evil?. . .

But Zedekiah the son of Chenaanah went near, and smote Micaiah on the cheek, and said, Which way went the Spirit of the Lord from me to speak unto thee?

And Micaiah said, Behold, thou shalt see in that day, when thou shalt go into an inner chamber to hide thyself.

And the king of Israel said, Take Micaiah, and...Put this fellow in the prison...until I come in peace.

And Micaiah said, If thou return at all in peace, the Lord hath not spoken by me....

...And the king of Israel disguised himself, and went into the battle....

And the battle increased that day: and the king was stayed up in his chariot against the Syrians, and died at even....

1 Kings 22:2,5-10,13-18,24-28,30,35

This is a story about religious politics. The king of Israel was a totally soulish king. He assembled all his dried-up, "pillow prophets." ("Pillow prophets" and "pillow preachers" always tell you what you *want* to hear so you won't leave their church or quit giving.) Then he said, "All right, you four hundred prophets who are supposed to hear from heaven — will we win or will we lose?" And all of them replied, "Yes, you will win!"

But the king of Judah, who knew God, didn't trust the pillow prophets. Something didn't seem right to him, so he said, "Well, that sounds like a good idea, but let's see what God has to say. Let's inquire of the Lord." This points out the difference between the two kings.

The king of Israel was into politics. People in politics don't like to inquire from heaven. They try to intimidate you by saying, "I heard from God. Why won't you listen to me?"

But the king of Judah refused to be intimidated. He insisted, "I don't think this is quite right. Isn't there another prophet around here whom we can inquire of? These prophets don't look too sharp to me."

You'd better know who's genuine and who's false. A phony prophecy comes across like a wet blanket. You want to leave the room. A genuine prophecy, on the other hand, comes across with a *force*. It contains structure, power, and meaning.

There was a genuine prophet — Micaiah — in Israel in those days. Notice they didn't even notify him that they were holding a meeting! They had to send an officer after him. When the officer arrived, he said, "All right, Micaiah, the four hundred prophets have said with one voice that we're going to win the battle. So why don't you say the same thing, and don't cause a problem like you usually do."

Micaiah had the right answer: "I will tell what God tells me." But between this reply and his utterance before the kings and the prophets, he changed. He told the kings, "Go up and prosper."

The king of Israel answered, "How many times have I told you to always tell me the truth in the name of the Lord?" Notice the word "times" (more than once).

So Micaiah replied, "All right, I'll tell you. Your plan is not of God. If you go out to war, you won't win, and the people will be scattered."

The king of Israel turned to the king of Judah and said, "See, I told you! He *always* says bad things about me!"

Then another prophet, who thought he was Mr. Hotshot, stepped up and slapped Micaiah! He sneered, "When did the Spirit of God leave *me* and tell *you* this?" He, too, tried to intimidate Micaiah, but Micaiah didn't back down. He said, "What I said *will* come to pass."

Then the king of Israel really got mad! He ordered, "Lock him up before he does anything else. Take him to prison! Get him out of my sight! Bind him!"

(Religious politicians *bind you* from flowing in the Spirit. They won't allow you to tell the truth the way God told you to tell it. They want you to merely "suggest" things.)

Micaiah's prophecy came to pass: The king of Israel was killed in battle that day.

The same thing is happening today in many religious circles around the world: Leaders who are playing religious politics won't allow ministers to preach the Gospel freely.

They won't allow prophets to prophesy the word of the Lord unless it's always bless, bless, bless, and more bless.

They won't allow anyone to bring a word of correction from God.

They won't allow anyone to convey the power of conviction that turns people's hearts toward God.

They only want things that will cause people's emotions to rejoice so they will think they've got it together when they haven't!

The prophet Jeremiah faced the same situation in his day, and he *nailed* the religious politicians. (Jer. 23.) He said, "You pillow prophets — all you say is, 'Peace, peace,' when there is no peace. And God is against you!" (I'd rather have man angry at me than God.)

Jeremiah said, "You prophesy things out of your own *heart*. You say you saw a vision when it was your own *head*. You're telling people there's going to be *peace* when there's going to be *war*. And you're telling people they're *fine* when they're *guilty* of worshipping themselves and their possessions.

"You're prophesying wrong — out of your own heart rather than out of the heart of heaven. God says, 'I am against you, and you shall be judged.' "

Jeremiah told the people not to listen to these false prophets. But Jeremiah didn't stop there; he even got onto the pastors. He said, "You pastors don't visit the sheep. You don't feed the sheep. You don't take care of them. You abuse them. Woe unto you!"

Religious politics destroys the heart of a man for his congregation. He becomes more concerned about his reputation than about the life of his sheep.

I've dealt with a few of these politicians behind closed doors. I've said, "Who do you think you are — God? You're walking in Hollywood Christianity. You make sure your bills are paid, but you don't have any true concern for your people!"

God has no *superstars;* He only has *servants.* If a servant does his job, God will promote him. But no matter how great his name may become, a servant will still have power to meet the needs of the people and help them when they're in trouble. That's what God's ministry gifts are for.

Characteristics of Religious Politicians

Now let me give you some characteristics of religious politicians.

1. Religious politicians are men-pleasers. They are more concerned about what men say about them than what God says about them. Galatians 1:10 says, **For do I now persuade men, or God? or do I seek to please men? for if I yet pleased men, I should not be the servant of Christ.**

I've known many great ministries that "died" before they were born. Why? Because you can't succeed in the world's way in God's kingdom. God doesn't put His glory on people who don't please Him. In other words, they have no power!

Religious politicians are manipulative; they *bind* you to themselves. In this hour, many are binding God's young servants and God's great men alike so they can't flow under the greatest anointing the world has ever seen. They're keeping revival from breaking out!

Ministers must get free and stay free from this manipulation! (However, there's nothing wrong with being committed to a church and its leaders if they're not trying to manipulate you.)

We must learn to recognize the wiles of the devil, as Paul said, **Lest Satan should get an advantage of us: for we are not ignorant of his devices** (2 Cor. 2:11).

2. Religious politicians try to gain influence by whom they know and what they've done. They're always worried about their reputation and their image.

They think they've got it together because they look sharp. They think that if you don't look like you've got it together *outwardly,* you don't have it together spiritually. They look wonderful in the soulish realm; everything they wear is first class. But first class is not necessarily Holy Spirit class! Yes, it's important to dress well, but believe me, if you're in right relationship with the Lord, you'll get it together.

Religious politicians are always talking about themselves and "their" ministry. "Me, myself, and I" are their trinity.

They try to gain influence by rubbing shoulders with important people. They think, "If I can just get close to this well-known minister, he will see my gift and connect me with the right people." *The only connection you need is with God.* When God sees fit to connect His servants, He'll connect you. Don't you try to do it. And if you are doing it, you're into religious politics.

I want *glorious connections* — connections that are brought about by and in the Holy

Spirit. The Bible says that it is God who causes one to rise and another to fall. The only reason you would fall is if you did something wrong, like become a religious politician.

God hates politics! When you get to heaven, there is no voting. You flow in the Spirit and obey!

I once asked God, "What is religious politics, and how does one enter into it?" He answered, "The first time you voice an opinion about something that's none of your business, you enter into the political arena. Even if it is your business, and you don't express it correctly, you have entered into the religious political scene." (In other words, if you don't want to be political, keep your mouth shut!)

When I studied Church history for six years, I learned that those who were the quietest were the most powerful. People who always have an opinion about something usually are of the wrong spirit. (It's called a busybody spirit!)

3. Religious politicians cause those involved in politics to compromise their calling, their

anointing. To keep the people's approval and support, religious politicians will water down what they know to be the truth.

I'd rather enjoy God's blessings upon my preaching than see your head nodding, "Amen," or rely upon your offerings. Your money won't put me over or cause me to go under. God is my Source. He called me; you didn't.

While it is true that ministers must walk in love, they must never compromise their calling or anointing. Operate under your anointing to its fullest strength, so people will receive its maximum benefit.

4. Religious politicians are notorious liars and cheaters. They're two-faced, lawless, and phony. Religious politicians will flatter you to your face and stab you in the back (or try to take over your church or ministry).

You can say something in a *natural* framework but project the wrong attitude in the *spiritual* realm. Religious politicians are wicked because they operate in *both* spheres: They're both intellectual and spiritual.

5. Religious politicians are power-hungry. They won't pay the price to get the true power from God. They like to be influential. They like to control and dominate. They believe that because they *seem* to be successful and have it all together, their natural achievements are the equivalent of God's approval. (But what God really approves of is having your spirit, soul, and body so in tune that they are able to flow accurately with the Holy Spirit.)

This is another reason why power-hungry people will accuse you of operating with false spirits when you begin to operate in the miraculous realm. They'll argue, "Well, *I've* got it together, and if God is going to use *anyone*, He'll surely use me."

The Bible says in Philippians 2:3, **Let nothing be done through strife or vainglory; but in lowliness of mind let each esteem other better than themselves.** Religious politicians *like* vainglory! Vainglory is carnal, fleshly admiration of people.

6. Religious politicians persuade their followers to work in the Name of God, but their work is done by human effort and strength, not by the will or the strength of God. And the Bible says that if the Lord doesn't build the house, it won't stand. (Matt. 15:13.)

In this hour, many ministries are falling apart internally. Soon this shall be evident even in the natural realm, and they shall collapse before the dawn of a new destiny appears. Don't be amazed when some of these religious structures collapse, because if they were not founded and built by the Spirit of God, they will not stand in the storms that are coming.

I like to state it this way: God didn't call Noah to build a luxury cruiser. Neither did He tell Noah to build a rubber raft. God told Noah to build an *ark* that would survive the waves and the storm.

Many ministers today are building luxury cruisers. Others are too lazy to build, so all they have is a rubber raft, and they wonder why God can't use them. It's because they're not building by the will and the power of God; they're building by human desire and human effort.

It won't work when a person tries to live in the realm of the Spirit by human effort. Have you ever seen those who try to "manufacture" false signs and wonders? I feel sorry for crippled people sometimes. They come to church and the minister tries to get them to walk, but there's no anointing there for their healing, because the minister didn't pray to get any. He watched television instead of seeking heaven, or he sought a promoter to promote him. When nothing happens, he accuses the crippled person of not having any faith!

I've got a question for you: How could Kathryn Kuhlman get up in front of 10,000 people — many of whom were skeptics, negative, curiosity-seekers, or devil-possessed — and while they were sitting there without a bit of faith, they got healed? Their healing didn't depend on their faith. It was because Miss Kuhlman obeyed God and walked in the glory.

Anyone can stand up and *sound* spiritual — but only those who pray and seek the face of God will come out with the Word of the Lord. You in the ministry need to get the *power* so that when you speak, it's *God* who is speaking, not you giving your little seven-point prosperity sermon.

If you don't get the true glory, you don't have a ministry. If you don't get the true power, nothing will happen. If you don't get the true Word of God, you have *nothing* to say. Quit trying to make everyone believe you're in a deep spiritual realm when you're really in a shallow one!

Some people try to act like they're way out in the Spirit. "Yes, I hear — and I'll obey," they say piously. Then they turn around and ask, "Who'll give me $20? Who'll give me $50?" Then they give you sob stories about non-existent orphanages or other projects. Later, when a legitimate servant of God who doesn't beg comes to town, the people have nothing left to give — and they wonder why they don't get a reward for their giving. Sons of God are supposed to be led by His Spirit.

I've been in meetings where offerings were being received for projects and God said, "I'm not in that. Don't give." I've said, "But Lord . . ." (You want to participate so you'll look good. If your friend gave $500, you should give $1,000. That's the way religious politicians act.)

7. Religious politicians surround themselves with "yes" men. They instill fear in them that if they don't follow what they say, they'll be out of the will of God. I don't like "yes" people. There's no power in them. Those who are looking for true counsel can't find it among "yes" people.

But religious politicians surround themselves with weak people who don't know much, so when they say, "Well, God told me to do thus and so," their "yes" people say, "That's right. We agree with you." If one person questions a decision, they get upset with him, even if he is right. Then they wonder why their organization isn't successful.

8. Religious politicians accuse those who live by God's Word and preach by the

anointing of the Spirit of being harsh, arrogant, and not walking in love. Why? Because religious politicians don't like confrontation; they like *approval*.

They do not like people who preach the truth boldly, bluntly, and accurately. The truth haunts them. It convicts them. They don't want to hear God's authoritative orders from a man or woman of God; they prefer bland, humanistic ministers who give "suggestions." They want ministers to walk in human sympathy, not in the love of God, which is truth.

Jesus came to heal the brokenhearted, to set the captives free, and to deliver people. But religious politicians keep you bound and dependent upon them. That's why a church may fall apart when a man of God passes from the scene. The church was dependent on the man; it wasn't built on the Rock of Jesus Christ. You don't build a church or ministry upon a personality; you build it upon the Rock, Christ Jesus.

Religious politicians also want to make you dependent upon their approval. They like to sit in the great judgment seat of ministries. After the service, they take you behind closed doors and say, "All right, we want to critique you. You shouldn't use words like 'sin' or 'repent.' We're old — we've been around a lot longer than you — and we want to help you."

Some will say, "I'm cautiously excited about your ministry." Others will try the sly approach: "We just want to *help* you. If you'd come and sit under our ministry, we'd help you be great." (They don't *have* a ministry.) Others will flatter you and try to get you to agree with them against another minister. (That's touching the anointing, Ps. 105:15.)

If young ministers don't recognize these words from religious politicians as an attack of the devil, it may hold back or totally annihilate their ministry — because there is great power in words.

9. Religious politicians are never transparent, even with their close friends. There's always an air of showmanship about them. They can never be themselves. They live

another life behind closed doors. They think you won't know it. Jesus was transparent, and we've got to be transparent too.

10. Religious politicians don't care about the people they hurt or destroy on their way to the top, as long as *they* get there. They will use and abuse you. Jesus reached the top, and He cared about Judas!

I'd like to ask religious politicians some questions: After you get to the top by stepping on everyone, who will your friends be? Who will be there to pray with you? How much will you enjoy your "success" then?

You'll never attain lasting success through religious politics. You'll never get to be big fast. *And what you compromise to gain, you will lose forever.* God still owns the top of the mountain — and He also owns the ladder that reaches it! To be truly successful, you've got to go through God's school of servanthood.

If your motives are not right, God can't accept your life as a sacrifice that is acceptable to Him. (Rom. 12.) The purity of ministry must return. *It's Jesus, Jesus, and more Jesus.* It's not Jesus and you. It's none of self and all of Him. God will only bless people who live like that.

11. Religious politicians are *talkers,* not *prayers*. People who pray have glory, anointing, and power. People are attracted to their meetings by *the glory* they carry as they preach; not by their *personality.* The glory they carry ministers to the hearts of the congregation without the minister ever knowing what is transpiring. Ministers are just doors for the glory of God to flow through — doors God comes through to be seen in the earth and prove His existence in the lives of people.

On the other hand, politicians just want to chitchat, talk, and make deals. God has no deals! He has no sales, either! You either pay full price, or you don't get the anointing!

You can talk people into confusion, but you can't talk them into the glory. You can only preach them into the glory by the anointing of the Holy Spirit.

People who don't pray are not worth listening to. People who don't pray won't make it.

God is not looking for a *politician;* He's looking for a prayerful soldier of the cross — someone who will "grab hold of the horns of the altar" and stay on his or her knees until heaven opens and the glory falls! We must have it!

12. Religious politicians give gifts to flatter and make inroads of control into your life and ministry. That's why I call them Mr. Big Bucks. Sometimes people give a great deal of money, thinking that entitles them to have a voice in running your life and ministry.

As a Christian, you live in a war, and you've got to keep watching for your enemy in his various disguises. If something shows up on your spiritual "radar" (your spirit), there's something there. People who live out of their head don't pick up things in their spirit. They don't know God very well. You only know *about* God by your head. Really knowing God comes from the heart.

13. Religious politicians tell lies about those who threaten their influence. You can preach a sermon, not knowing what the people are involved in, hit their sins head-on, and scare

them. The next thing you know, they're trying to ruin your life and ministry, accusing you of doing things you've never done — all because you hit too close to the truth.

In conclusion, how can you stay free from religious politics? First, make yourself lose all natural desire to be known, respected, or popular.

Ministry is not for the sake of how famous you can become or how much money you can accumulate. Ministry is meant to help people find Jesus and grow strong. The ministry is not a matter of choosing an occupation; it's becoming a servant!

In time, as you are faithful in the ministry, God may give you a big ministry. Those who don't *want* a big ministry usually *get* one! People involved in politics can't understand it. It's called a work of the Holy Spirit!

Second, to keep out of religious politics, remember that the purpose of ministry is to introduce people to Jesus, the King of kings and the Lord of lords. So keep your heart focused on God, and keep introducing people to Jesus.

Also, don't become discouraged by those who seem to be succeeding quickly through political means. Often, those who are paying the legitimate price are discouraged by phonies who show up with some new "revelation" that isn't Biblical, yet people pump thousands of dollars into their ministry. If you're not careful, you may feel like you're not accomplishing anything — yet you're worth far more than those "rocket" ministers who will suddenly explode or disappear.

What matters to me is to get the presence of God into the Church. I want to see His *power* so manifested that it will shake and rearrange all of us so that we become more like Jesus!

For ministry information, please contact:

Roberts Liardon
P.O. Box 30710
Laguna Hills, CA 92654

Please include your prayer requests and comments when you write.

BOOKS BY ROBERTS LIARDON

Kathryn Kuhlman
A Spiritual Biography of God's Miracle Working Power
Run to the Battle
Learning To Say No Without Feeling Guilty
I Saw Heaven
A Call to Action
The Invading Force
The Quest for Spiritual Hunger
Breaking Controlling Powers
Religious Politics
Cry of the Spirit
Spiritual Timing

VIDEOS BY ROBERTS LIARDON

I Saw Heaven
God's Explosive Weapons
The Roar of the '90s
The Sword of Gideon
Developing an Excellent Spirit
No More Walls
Confronting the Brazen Heavens
Invasion '91 (10-tape series)
Reformers and Revivalists (5-volume series)
God's Generals
(8-volume set of tapes, 60 minutes each)

Additional copies of this book and other books and videos, are available from your local bookstore or by contacting:

Embassy Publishing
P.O. Box 3500 • Laguna Hills, CA 92654

Roberts Liardon was born in Tulsa, Oklahoma. He was born again, baptized in the Holy Spirit, and called to the ministry at the age of eight, after being caught up to heaven by the Lord Jesus.

Roberts was powerfully commissioned by the Lord to study the lives of God's great men and women ministers, to know why they succeeded and why they failed. The following six years were spent in preparation for that calling and for the vision which God had given him.

In his teens, Roberts began preaching and teaching in various churches — denominational and non-denominational alike — Bible colleges and universities. He has traveled extensively in the United States and Canada over the past few years.

Roberts' missions outreaches have taken him to Africa, Europe, and Asia. Ministering the Gospel with great anointing from God and the power of the Holy Spirit, Roberts challenges people to walk in the Spirit.